Earth

Donna Walsh Shepherd

Watts LIBRARY™

Franklin Watts
A Division of Scholastic Inc.
New York • Toronto • London • Auckland • Sydney
Mexico City • New Delhi • Hong Kong
Danbury, Connecticut

For Chadney Shepherd, Shane Shepherd, and Aaron Shepherd,
who mean the world to me

Note to readers: Definitions for words in **bold** can be found in the Glossary at the back of this book.

Photographs © 2002: Corbis Images: 51 (Todd Gipstein), 26, 27 (Paul A. Souders); Hulton Archive/Getty Images/Smithsonian Institution/Reuters: 4; NASA: cover, 3 left, 7, 8, 30, 39, 41, 42, 44, 45, 49, 52, 53; Photo Researchers, NY: 3 right, 12, (Julian Baum/SPL), 18, 19 (Sally Bensusen/SPL), 3, 28 (Tony Craddock/SPL), 23 (Carl Frank), 15, 16 (David Hardy/SPL), 36 (David Nunuk/SPL), 40, 43 (John Sanford/SPL), 34 (Frank Zullo); Photri Inc.: 18 left, 46, 54; The Image Works/ Joe Carini: 24.

Illustration on page 22 by Bernard Adnet.

Solar system diagram created by Greg Harris.

The photograph on the cover shows a digital image of Earth from space.

Library of Congress Cataloging-in-Publication Data

Walsh Shepherd, Donna.
 Earth / Donna Walsh Shepherd.
  p. cm. — (Watts library)
  Summary: Describes Earth's creation, plate tectonics, atmosphere, climate, and moon, as well as how life developed on the planet.
  Includes bibliographical references and index.
  ISBN 0-531-12043-0 (lib. bdg.) 0-531-15559-5 (pbk.)
  1. Earth—Juvenile literature. [1. Earth.] I. Title. II. Series.

QB631.4 .W37 2002
525—dc21   2002007536

Contents

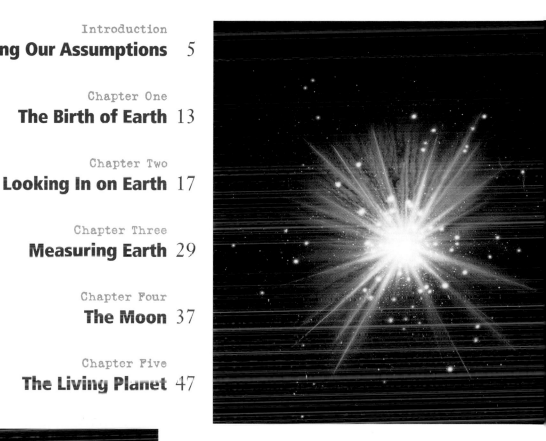

This second-century model of the universe by Claudius Ptolemy illustrates the mistaken assumption that Earth is at the center of the universe.

Changing Our Assumptions

A thousand years ago, during the Dark Ages, the world's best scientists thought they knew some things about **Planet Earth** for certain. They believed that Earth was a flat disk under the dome of the sky. They believed that Earth was the center of the universe, and the Sun, Moon, and stars all circled it. People who offered different theories about Earth's place in the heavens were ridiculed or even imprisoned. In those times new knowledge and different ideas were considered threatening to the belief that God had placed Earth in the center of the universe for the benefit of humankind.

Today we work eagerly to gain new knowledge and to answer questions about Earth and the universe. We know that Earth is shaped like a sphere, not a disk, and it is certainly not the center of the universe. Earth is part of a system of planets revolving around a rather average star that we call a sun. Our sun is located in a rotating disk of many stars. This great cluster of stars is called the Milky Way **Galaxy**. Our sun is only one of 300 billion stars in the Milky Way. Beyond the Milky Way are billions of other galaxies, each with billions of stars.

From the distance of space, our solar system of nine known planets appears insignificant, only a small part of a very large galaxy. Four small rocky planets **orbit** in oval patterns around the Sun. Beyond them orbit four more planets that are much larger and mostly composed of gases. Beyond the last large planet, Neptune, a few rocky objects are also caught in the Sun's gravitational pull. One is the ninth planet, Pluto.

Earth, the third planet from the Sun, is slightly larger than the second (Venus) and almost twice the size of the fourth (Mars). It is a bit flattened at the poles, and it bulges in the center, just below the equator. Earth is the nearest planet to the Sun to have its own **satellite**, the Moon. Most planets' moons are very small compared to the planet itself, but not Earth's moon. It is so large that scientists have classified Earth and the Moon as a twin planet system.

Earth's moon is so
large that Earth and
its satellite are
classified as a twin
planet system.

From space, Planet Earth appears in vivid colors of brown, green, blue, and white. It looks quite different from its neighboring planets, most of which are swirling orange and red.

From space, Earth looks quite different from the other eight planets. Instead of appearing swirling orange and red like its neighbors Mercury, Mars, and Jupiter, Earth is a deep blue with masses of brown and mottled green and white splotches. Sprinkled through the splotches are telescopes and satellites gathering information about Earth and the universe. Although we cannot see it from the outskirts of the solar system, Earth's blue oceans, brown and green land, and moist white clouds house a wide variety of living things. We often refer to Earth as the Living Planet.

Through the use of new technology, people can see, measure, and understand Earth in ways not possible a thousand years ago, a hundred years ago, or even ten years ago. As we have gathered new knowledge, many of the old assumptions about Earth have been proven wrong. Although Earth is not the center of the universe, it is the central location from which we learn about the universe—the beginning point of exploring our space neighborhood. Because we know Earth best, our planet is the standard by which we measure and try to understand all other objects in space.

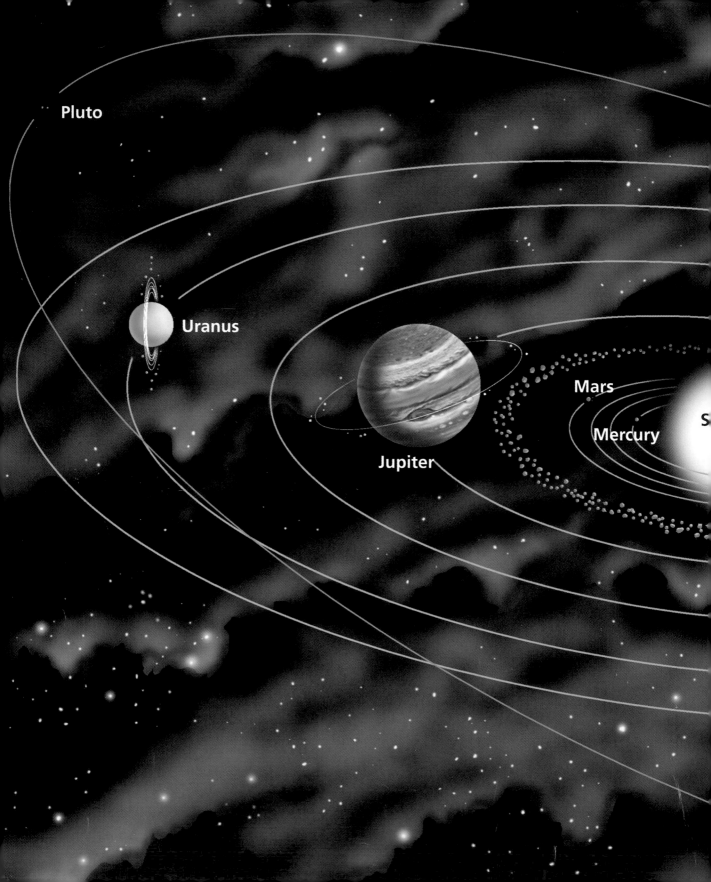

The Solar System

Venus

Moon

Earth

Asteroid Belt

Saturn

Neptune

Pictured here is an artist's impression of the Big Bang, the great explosion that gave birth to the universe. The white spots are giant clouds of gas and dust called nebulas, which have already started forming into galaxies.

Chapter One

The Birth of Earth

About thirteen billion years ago, nothing at all existed—not planets, not people, not even time or space. Suddenly, in that emptiness, in one moment shorter than a second, everything changed. At a point smaller than a grain of sand, a giant explosion of energy sent light, heat, and tiny **atoms** spinning outward and colliding. This powerful explosion created temperatures of more than 18 million degrees Fahrenheit (10 million degrees Celsius). We call it the Big Bang.

Scientists do not know how or why the Big Bang happened, but they believe it was the beginning of our universe as we understand it. After the explosion, over billions of years, great clouds of gases and dust formed in space. In these **nebulas**, stars and galaxies are born. All objects in the universe, including our solar system and Planet Earth, are still moving away from that point of explosion.

A Solar System Spin-off

About 4.6 billion years ago, a star exploded in our galaxy. This caused the nebulas nearby to swirl together. Inside the spinning clouds, **gravity** began pulling particles toward the center. As the bombarding hot gas particles hit each other in the center of the cloud, they built up enormous levels of heat. This became a star, our sun.

As the Sun formed at the cloud's center, the rest of the cloud formed a flat disk around it. Clumps of dust and gases called **planetesimals** orbited in the outer parts of the cloud. Over time, the planetesimals combined to make bigger clumps that eventually formed into planets. While they were forming, Earth and the other planets were frequently bombarded by **meteorites** and **comets**. These objects brought new material to the planets, including some water.

Now our solar system has nine known planets, several moons, an asteroid belt, and a few comets. All of these objects orbit the Sun. Earth and the solid inner planets are made mostly of oxygen, iron, silicon, and magnesium. The outer

Celestial Names

Stars and planets are often named for gods from Greek and Roman mythology. Planet Earth is named for Terra Mater, the Roman goddess Mother Earth. It is also called Gaea, the name of the Greek Earth goddess. The modern English word *earth* comes from an ancient English word meaning ground or dirt.

planets, called the gas giants, contain gases such as hydrogen, helium, and methane around a small rocky core. Earth orbits on a path about 93 million miles (150,000 kilometers) away from the Sun.

Planetesimals combined with bits of dust and pieces of rock as they orbited the Sun and eventually formed into planets.

Earth Begins to Shape Up

After its initial materials gathered into a hot sphere, Earth began to cool. Vents and volcanoes on the planet's surface released streams of gases, mostly hydrogen, nitrogen, and carbon dioxide. This steam, held close to Earth by gravity, became our **atmosphere**.

After plantlike organisms began growing on Earth, they released oxygen into the atmosphere. The atoms of oxygen combined with atoms of hydrogen to create **water vapor**. As the water vapor cooled below boiling (212°F or 100°C), it began to rain—and rain, and rain. It did not stop raining for a million years. When it did stop, the outer edge of Earth's **mantle** had cooled to rock, and great bodies of water flowed in low places.

Making Water

The chemical name, or formula, for water is H_2O because two atoms of hydrogen gas (H) combine with one atom of oxygen gas (O) to make a molecule of water.

15

This cutaway illustration shows the five main layers of Earth: inner core, outer core, mantle (separated into two sublayers), and crust. The top part of the mantle shows convection patterns near the crust's plates.

Chapter Two

Looking In on Earth

As Earth cooled, the heaviest materials, iron and nickel, sank to the center. Silicon, a lighter material, rose to the surface. Gases, the lightest materials of all, floated above the rocky sphere. Eventually Earth settled into five main layers. The outer layer is the atmosphere, the envelope of gases that surrounds Earth. The top layer of Earth is the crust, the layer of rock and water that we live on. Below the crust is the mantle, a layer of hot rock. In the center of Earth are the outer core and the inner core. The outer core is mostly hot liquid iron, and the inner core is hot solid iron.

The Thin Blue Blanket

Separating Earth's surface from space is its atmosphere, the layers of gases that surround a planet or a moon. Our atmosphere provides the air we breathe, protects us from the Sun, keeps us warm like a blanket, and allows life-sustaining rains to form. Astronauts say that from space our atmosphere looks like a thin blue blanket. The main part of Earth's atmosphere is about as thick as the thickest part of Earth's crust—50 miles (80 km).

Our atmosphere is mostly nitrogen gas (78 percent). Oxygen, which animals need in order to breathe, makes up

Earth's atmosphere looks like a thin blue blanket in this striking space shuttle picture of sunrise over the Amazon River basin.

only 21 percent of the atmosphere. Argon gas makes up 0.93 percent. Dust and water vapor are also suspended in the atmosphere. These gases thin out as they get farther and farther away from Earth. About 600 miles (970 km) away from Earth, the atmosphere thins into nothing.

Layers of Atmosphere

Just as Earth has layers, the atmosphere also has layers. Of the four main layers, the closest to Earth's surface is the troposphere. This is the layer of air we breathe, where airplanes fly, and where weather forms. Strong winds called jet streams flow over the surface of the troposphere. The troposphere varies from 6 miles (10 km) thick at the poles to 10 miles (16 km) thick at the equator. At the upper edge of the troposphere,

This illustration identifies the atmosphere's layers by the activities that occur in them. Weather occurs in the troposphere (lower left), which is also where passenger airplanes fly. Above is the stratosphere (hot air balloon), where the ozone layer is found. Meteor showers occur in the mesosphere (lower center). Above, in the thermosphere (space shuttle), auroras occur. At right are electromagnetic radiation, gamma rays (center right, pale blue), X rays, ultraviolet rays, a rainbow, infrared rays (orange), and radio waves (red).

called the **tropopause**, there are clouds of ice crystals as cold as −112°F (−80°C).

The Earth absorbs heat from the Sun and releases the warmth into the troposphere at night. Greenhouse gases, such as carbon dioxide, in this layer help block heat from escaping back into space. These gases help maintain an appropriate temperature for the existence of life on Earth. High concentrations of these gases can overheat Earth, however. Scientists have shown that excessive burning of fossil fuels such as coal and petroleum has increased the amount of carbon dioxide in the troposphere. This has led to global warming.

The next layer is the stratosphere. It extends from the tropopause to 30 miles (50 km) above Earth. In the lower part of the stratosphere is the ozone layer. Ozone gas absorbs the Sun's deadly ultraviolet rays. Life on Earth could not exist without the ozone layer. This is why many people are concerned that large holes in the ozone are growing over the poles, and the layer is thinning at mid-latitude regions.

Beyond the stratosphere is the mesosphere. This layer extends from the top of the stratosphere to 50 miles (80 km) above Earth. The mesosphere is a layer of decreasing **density** and increasing coldness. Strong winds blow here. When meteors hit this layer, they usually burn and become shooting stars. Together, the troposphere, the stratosphere, and the mesosphere make up 99 percent of Earth's atmosphere.

The last layer is the thermosphere. In this layer the air is extremely thin—so thin that **air pressure**, the weight or

Losing the Ozone

Ozone (O_3) is a gas whose molecules are made of three bonded atoms of oxygen. Some chemical pollutants put into the atmosphere by humans can interact with ozone and destroy it. When chemicals such as chloro-fluorocarbon (CFC) molecules hit ozone molecules, one of the three atoms of oxygen is knocked away. The carbon from CFCs combines with the remaining two atoms of ozone to create carbon dioxide gas. This ties up the oxygen atoms so that ozone cannot form. Without sufficient ozone, the Sun's ultraviolet rays are not absorbed. Exposure to ultraviolet rays is a leading cause of skin cancer. Sources of CFC pollutants include refrigerators, freezers, air conditioners, and aerosol sprays.

downward push of the air, is one hundred times less than it is at sea level. The thermosphere extends to about 300 miles (480 km) above Earth. Unlike the other layers of the atmosphere, its main gases are hydrogen and helium. The northern and southern lights, also called the **auroras**, appear in this layer.

At the edge of the thermosphere is the exosphere. This is where the atmosphere ends. Uninterrupted by Earth's gravitational pull, solar winds—the charged particles emitted by the Sun—sweep past Earth into space.

Layers of Earth

When they first formed, Earth's oceans and land were very different from the way they are today. There was only one piece of land, a giant continent we call Pangaea, and one great ocean, Panthalassa. It took billions of years for the continents

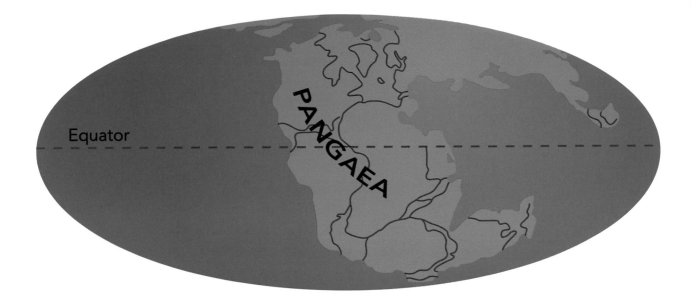

Equator

PANGAEA

The land on Earth used to consist of one large continent called Pangaea.

to separate into their current forms. Earth continues to change, and our planet will look very different a million years from now.

The crust layer is our home on Earth. There are two types of crust—the oceanic crust, which lies under the oceans, and the continental crust, which forms the land masses. The crust is so thin relative to the rest of Earth that it can be compared

Recycling Earth's Crust

Although many meteors and comets hit Earth in its early history, few impact craters are visible on its surface. This is because Earth recycles its outer crust material. **Molten** rock from inside Earth oozes out of cracks in the oceanic crust. As it flows upward, it pushes the plates of crust outward. In other parts of the world, this pressure causes the crust to fold back down into the mantle, where it melts in the intense heat. Earthquakes and volcanoes that form along these fold lines either bury or break apart Earth's surface. Rain, frost, and sunlight also erode, or wear away, Earth's rocky crust. The recycling of Earth's crust is a slow, constant process.

to a peel on an apple. It averages only about 5 miles (8 km) thick underneath Earth's oceans and 25 miles (40 km) underneath the surface of the land. The crust's total area is nearly 200 million square miles (500 million square km). Only 29 percent of that amount consists of continental crust; water covers 71 percent of the crust. Just the top few inches of the continental crust consists of soil; the rest is rock. The crust is not a solid layer. Instead, it floats on the mantle below like puzzle pieces. These large sections of crust are called plates.

Although they cannot see under the crust, scientists are able to study the interior of the Earth. One way is through earthquakes. Earthquakes send waves moving through the ground, just as a rock thrown into a lake sends waves moving out over the water. As an earthquake's seismic waves travel down through solid rock to soft rock or liquid, they slow down and may bend in a different direction. The movement of waves tells scientists a great deal about what lies under Earth's crust.

Scientists can learn a lot about Earth's crust by studying earthquakes.

23

*The magma that
fuels volcanoes comes
from Earth's mantle.*

Underneath the crust lies the mantle. This layer of rock is 1,800 miles (2,900 km) thick. Its temperature ranges from 1,600°F (870°C) at the cooler top to 8,000°F (4,400°C) in the depths. The upper portion of the mantle contains pockets of **magma**, a material made up of molten rock, crystallized minerals, and gases. Some of these pockets of magma fuel volcanoes. Deeper into the mantle, the hot rock is solid. Although the mantle is solid, pressure from above causes some areas to slowly move around.

Next is the outer core, a 1,400-mile (2,250-km) layer of very hot liquid iron with a trace of nickel. The outer core's temperature ranges from about 9,000°F (5,000°C) on the upper edge to about 11,000°F (6,100°C) at the lower edge. In places, the upper edge of the outer core has formed a mushy crust next to the mantle. Heat and radioactive material decaying in this layer cause the molten iron to circulate around the solid inner core at a rate of about 0.25 inch (0.5 cm) per second. This movement causes currents of electricity to flow through the iron and creates a **magnetic field** around Earth.

The inner core is made of solid iron and some nickel. Its diameter measures 800 miles (1,300 km), about the size of the Moon. It is even hotter than the outer core—about 13,000°F (8,000°C). Although this temperature is hot enough to melt iron, the inner core is solid. Pressure from the other layers pushing down upon the inner core causes the hot iron to solidify. The inner core is slowly growing as the outer core's liquid iron attaches to it and solidifies under pressure.

Taking Earth's Temperature

Generally speaking, the temperature inside Earth goes up about 1°F (0.56°C) for every 60 feet (18 meters) you go toward the core.

Earth's Magnetic Field

The outer core of Earth is made of charged liquid iron. This causes Earth to act like a magnet and to have a magnetic field. The magnetic field, or magnetosphere, around the Earth protects it from harmful radiation and particles from the Sun. As charged particles called the solar winds flow from the Sun

The northern lights (aurora borealis) sweep across the thermosphere above Earth.

toward Earth, they hit the magnetic field, and some are repelled and sweep by. Other solar wind particles are caught in the magnetic field and rapidly travel from pole to pole until they burn up or attach to other particles and become harmless. This happens about 50 miles (80 km) up in the atmosphere. When the trapped particles are plentiful, we see auroras, the northern and southern lights. Jupiter, Saturn, Uranus, and Earth are the only planets in our solar system with magnetic fields.

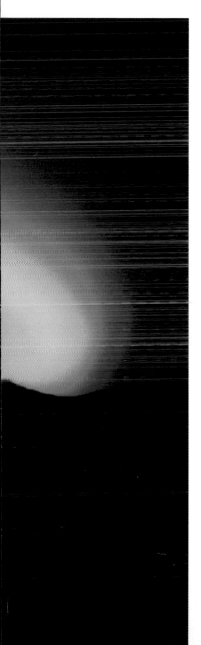

Like bar magnets, Earth has a positive and a negative charge. These are the north and south magnetic poles, which are near, but not at, the geographic North and South Poles. This charge causes compasses to point north. Scientists think that some animals, especially birds, use Earth's magnetic field to guide them along their migration routes. They seem to sense direction and distance by the strength of the pull of the magnetic north pole. These animals appear to have their own internal compasses.

Earth's Compass

By studying rocks, scientists have discovered that Earth's positive and negative charges have switched poles several times in Earth's history. We have no idea why or how this happens.

Scientists use their measurements of Earth as a basis for understanding the rest of the universe.

Chapter Three

Measuring Earth

Scientists have many different ways of measuring Earth and other objects in space. They base all their measurements on Earth. This provides a comparison for understanding strange and distant places. Common things that scientists study are gravity, **volume**, **mass**, density, time, and distance.

Gravity

Gravity is the force that causes anything with mass (matter) to attract other objects

Earth's gravity keeps the Moon in orbit.

How Earth Measures Up

Distance from the Sun: 91 million to 95 million miles (146 million to 153 million km)—it ranges because Earth orbits in an oval shape

Average circumference: 24,902 miles (40,075 km)

Average diameter: 7,926 miles (12,750 km)

Land: 29.1 percent

Ocean: 70.9 percent

Average year-round temperature: 57°F (14°C)

Extreme temperatures: 136°F (56°C) Libya, Africa; −128.6°F (−89.6°C) Antarctica

Average land height: 0.5 mile (1 km) above sea level

Average ocean depth: 2 miles (3.5 km)

Highest land point: Mount Everest, 29,028 feet (8,848 m)

Lowest land point: Dead Sea shore, 1,310 feet (399 m) below sea level

with mass. The larger and more dense a body's mass, the stronger its force of gravity. All celestial bodies have gravity, sometimes called gravitational pull or a gravitational field. Even people have their own gravity, but it is relatively insignificant because of their small size. Earth's strong gravity holds objects to Earth and keeps the Moon in its orbit. The Sun has a much stronger gravitational pull than Earth does. It holds Earth and the other eight planets in its orbit.

We measure gravity by the amount of downward pull on an object at Earth's sea level. At sea level, gravity equals 1 G-force. We compare the gravity of other space objects to this. On Earth, in 1 G-force, a 100-pound person weighs 100 pounds. If that person were to travel to the Moon, which has much weaker gravity, that person would weigh only 17 pounds. The

Moon has only about 0.2 G-force. Venus has slightly less than 1 G-force, and a 100-pound person would weigh 88 pounds. On Jupiter, with its 2.4 G-forces, that same person would weigh 240 pounds.

Sizing Up Earth by Volume, Mass, and Density

The different things we measure on Earth and the other planets allow us to compare and contrast many different things about them. Volume is the amount of space an object fills. Earth's volume is 260 billion cubic miles (1.08 trillion cubic km). We often measure other space objects by how many Earths would fit into them. Earth is the middle-sized planet—four planets are smaller and four are larger.

Mass is the amount of material or matter in an object. Earth has $5,974 \times 10^{18}$ metric tons of matter. Pluto has only two-thousandths (0.0022) the mass of Earth, while Jupiter has 318 times Earth's mass.

Density is how tightly an object's material is packed together. A foam ball has more air space and less mass and density than a baseball of the same size. Wood floats because it is less dense than water. Density is measured by weight in grams per cubic centimeter at sea level, so the ocean's surface has a density of 1 gm/cm^3. Earth's average density is 5.5 gm/cm^3, but its density varies greatly from place to place. The density of the iron core is 7.87; the mantle's density is 3.3. The continental crust, which is largely granite, has a density of 2.58, while the oceanic crust is a bit denser, at 3 gm/cm^3.

All the rocky planets are much more dense and have much more mass for their size than the giant gaseous planets, whose matter is lightweight and loosely packed together. Earth is the densest planet in our solar system and has the greatest mass compared to size.

Measuring Time and Distance

On Earth we measure days, hours, and even minutes by dividing the length of Earth's orbit and rotation. Earth takes 365.25 days to complete one orbit around the Sun. This is how we measure a year. As Earth orbits the Sun, it also spins on its **axis**. We call one complete spin one day. This complete spin takes exactly 23.934 hours. When we divide a day into hours, minutes, and seconds, we are really marking the movement of Earth around the Sun. Because our division does not precisely match Earth's movement, we add one day on to the calendar every four years—every leap year—to keep the balance of time to rotation.

The Tilt of Earth

As Earth moves around the Sun in an elliptical pattern—an oval shape—it does not stand "up" straight in space. It tilts at a 23.5° angle. This gives Earth seasons. In winter, the northern hemisphere tilts away from the Sun. In summer, it tilts toward the Sun.

Rotating Around the Galaxy

Just as Earth and the other planets orbit the Sun, the Sun and our entire solar system orbit the center of the Milky Way Galaxy. The Sun is in a spiraling branch of stars about three-fourths away from center, toward the galaxy's edge. It takes the Sun 200 million Earth years to complete one orbit around the center of the Milky Way.

When we talk about time on other planets, we talk about Earth time. We refer to space time as Earth days or Earth years. A Mars year, or the time it takes Mars to rotate once around the Sun, equals 687 Earth days. One Saturn year is equivalent to 29.5 Earth years.

Measures of distance and time in space are often too great to be measured in relationship to Earth. To make the numbers easier to handle, scientists sometimes measure things by AUs, or Astronomical Units. One AU is the distance from Earth to the Sun—about 93 million miles (150 million km). Pluto is nearly 40 AUs from the Sun, which means it is 40 times farther away from the Sun than Earth is. Scientists usually measure great distances by how fast light travels through space. Light travels 186,000 miles (300,000 km) each second. Sunlight travels the 93 million miles (150 million km) to Earth in 8 minutes. It takes more than four Earth years for the Sun's light to travel to Earth. Although these are called light years, they measure distance rather than time. They represent how far light travels in an Earth year—about 6.25 trillion miles (10 trillion km). This means that our nearest star in the Milky Way Galaxy is 25 trillion miles (40 trillion km) away.

A mysterious full moon rises over water on Vancouver Island, Canada.

Chapter Four

The Moon

The mysteries of the Moon have inspired poets and scientists alike. The more we learn about our nearest celestial neighbor, the more fascinating it becomes for anyone who has watched the sliver of a crescent moon grow into a giant golden ball hanging low on the horizon. The Moon's features have romantic names such as Sea of Tranquillity, Bay of Rainbows, and Lake of Dreams. Up close, however, the Moon appears barren, dusty, and dead. It has no atmosphere, no weather, no water, no life. Still, Earth's satellite holds plenty of mystery and, for the lucky few who have visited it, delight.

Why We Have a Moon

Earth is the closest planet to the Sun to have a moon. Earth's Moon is much larger and closer to its planet than other moons in the solar system. After astronauts brought back the first moon rock samples, scientists learned that some of the Moon's rocks are quite similar to Earth's and some are quite different.

Using moon rocks, evidence found on Earth, and computer models, scientists theorized that 4.3 million years ago, Earth was hit by a newly forming planet about the size of Mars (half as big as Earth). This collision fractured off a piece of Earth and shattered the other object. Some of the debris stayed on Earth and some vaporized, but much of the flying debris from the collision got caught in Earth's gravitational field and began orbiting Earth. Over millions of years, Earth regained its spherical shape and the debris gathered together to form a new sphere—a moon caught in Earth's orbit.

Luna

The Moon is named after Luna, Roman goddess of the moon.

How the Moon Measures Up

Average distance from Earth: 238,860 miles (384,400 km)
Diameter: 2,160 miles (3,476 km), one-quarter that of Earth
Circumference: 6,790 miles (10,927 km)
Temperature: 230°F (110°C) in sunlight, –280°F (–140°C) in darkness
Average speed orbiting Earth: 2,300 miles (3,700 km) per hour
Time to complete one orbit of Earth: 27 days, 7 hours, 43 minutes
Volume: 5.2 billion cubic miles (21.7 billion cubic km), one-fiftieth that of Earth
Density: 3.34 gm/cm³ (60 percent of Earth's)
Atmosphere: none

The Moon's Surface

As the Moon formed, it was hit time after time by meteorites and meteoroids. All of this shows on its surface. Impact craters and *maria* (Latin for seas) cover most of the Moon's surface. These are not seas of water as early astronomers thought. Instead, they are hardened flows of lava from volcanoes or cracks in the Moon's crust.

Daedalus, one of the Moon's many craters, has a diameter of 50 miles (80 km).

Where Did All Our Craters Go?

It might seem odd that the Moon is covered with craters while Earth has so few. Early Earth was also heavily hit with meteorites, but Earth's crater marks have mostly eroded away from the effects of water, wind, and the movement of the crust's plates. Because the Moon has no atmosphere, it has neither wind nor water, so its craters remain. One of the best-known craters in the United States is Meteor Crater in eastern Arizona (pictured here). It is about 1 mile (1.6 km) across. The Moon has more than 500,000 craters larger than Meteor Crater. The largest is the Imbrium Basin, at 700 miles (1,100 km) across. When people see the face of the "man in the moon," the Imbrium Basin forms one of the eyes.

Other lunar features include mountain ranges and **rilles**, long valleys that were probably created by rivers of lava. The youngest lava flows on the Moon are more than two billion years old. The Moon is covered with dust and rock pieces called **regolith**. Some of the newest marks on the Moon's surface are astronauts' footprints in this dust. Because there is no wind or rain, the footprints will remain visible for many years.

Edwin E. Aldrin, Jr., stands by an American flag on the surface of the Moon on July 20, 1969. The tracks of his boots appear prominently in the Moon's regolith.

The Earth-Moon System

Many planets in our solar system have moons, but no other moon is as close to its planet, or as large in comparative size, as our moon is to Earth. Together, Earth and the Moon form a double planet system called the Earth-Moon system. They orbit around the Sun together on a common axis called the **barycenter**. This center point of the Earth-Moon system is located inside Earth, about halfway between the core and the crust.

As the Moon orbits Earth, it slowly rotates. It takes about 27.3 days for the Moon to orbit Earth, and it takes the same

The Galileo *spacecraft captured this photograph of the Moon in orbit around Earth from a distance of 3.9 million miles (6.2 million km) on December 16, 1992.*

The Moon's Phases

Moonshine is sunlight reflected off the Moon's surface. How much light we see reflected by the Moon depends on where it is in its orbit around Earth. If the Moon is between the Sun and Earth, we do not see any reflected light. This is called a new moon. As the Moon moves in its orbit, it reflects more and more sunlight toward Earth. First we see the sliver of a crescent moon and then a quarter moon. When the Moon has orbited halfway so that Earth is between the Moon and the Sun, we see a full moon—the full face reflecting light. As the Moon orbits back toward the Sun, it reflects less and less light. An increasing amount of reflection is called a waxing moon; a decreasing amount is a waning moon.

27.3 days for the Moon to rotate once. This means that the same side of the Moon always faces Earth, and we never see the far side. In 1959, Soviet space probes took the first pictures of the far side of the Moon. Now, like the near side, it has been completely photographed and mapped.

The gravitational pull of the Moon is gradually slowing Earth's rotation. This is causing the length of an Earth day to increase 16 seconds every million years. Rock evidence shows that 900 million years ago, an Earth day was only 19 hours long, and a year took 460 days.

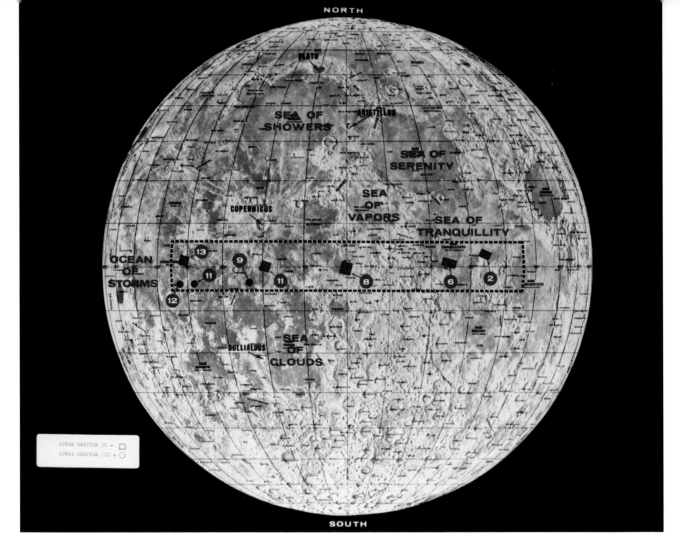

SEA OF
SHOWERS

ARISTILLUS

SEA OF
SERENITY

COPERNICUS

SEA
OF
VAPORS

SEA OF
TRANQUILLITY

OCEAN
OF
STORMS

BULLIALDUS

SEA
OF
CLOUDS

LUNAR ORBITER II - □
LUNAR ORBITER III - ○

This diagram, superimposed on an image of the Moon, shows eight possible landing sites for the first Apollo mission.

Visiting the Moon

Before 1969, when something was hopelessly impossible, people often said, "You might as well want water from the Moon." Then, on July 20, 1969, the first astronauts landed on the Moon. Almost the entire world watched on television as Neil Armstrong and Ed Aldrin became the first people to step onto the Moon's surface. Suddenly, nothing seemed impossible anymore.

John W. Young, an astronaut on the Apollo 16 *mission, explores the Moon in the Lunar Roving Vehicle on April 23, 1972.*

Visiting the Moon was one of the most exciting events in modern history. From 1969 to 1972, astronauts landed on the Moon six times. Twelve people have walked on the Moon and looked out to see a large blue Earth low in the sky. On each trip, the astronauts conducted research and collected lunar samples.

Moon rocks, lunar research, and astronauts' experiences have taught us much about the origins and history of Earth and the Moon, living in space, the effects of gravity, and far more. Using satellite information, water has been discovered frozen in the ground at the Moon's south pole. Now there is talk of someday using that water source to support a base on the Moon for exploration into space.

Touching the Moon

A small piece of black moon rock is on exhibit in the Air and Space Museum of the Smithsonian in Washington, D.C. There everyone may see a piece of the Moon up close and even touch it for good luck.

Scientists have yet to find another planet that hosts complex life forms. Here, a giraffe and a zebra refresh themselves at a water hole on the African grasslands.

Chapter Five

The Living Planet

Although our place in the universe is not as central as our ancestors believed, Planet Earth is still extraordinary. That blue sphere is far enough from the Sun to be warm—neither hot like Venus, at 864°F (462°C), nor cold like Mars, at –225°F (–143°C). At an average temperature of 57°F (14°C), Earth is a perfect place for life to thrive. It is the only place we know of with a temperature range that allows water to exist in all three forms—vapor, liquid, and ice.

Clues to the Beginning of Life

Scientists think that life on Earth began in warm, shallow seas. These mineral-rich waters are called the Primordial Soup—the cooking pot of early life. About 3.5 billion years ago, carbon, oxygen, hydrogen, and amino acids began a reaction that started the chain of life. Scientists are not sure how this happened. Some speculate that chemicals essential to start life arrived from outer space in a meteorite. Other scientists think that lightning or the Sun's radiation might have sparked the chain of life. Whatever happened, it was a complex process.

One clue about early life is found deep in the ocean. Hot, mineral-rich water flows out of cracks in the ocean floor, and the minerals pile up like chimneys around the waterspouts. Primitive bacteria live on the chimneys and eat the minerals. Worms, crabs, snails, and other tiny creatures feed on the bacteria. Scientists think that this tiny ecosystem may be duplicating the development pattern of early life on Earth.

We do not know if Earth is unique in the universe, or even in the Milky Way, but no other object in our solar system has been host to such a wide variety of life forms. It is possible that bacteria or other basic forms of life exist elsewhere in our solar system. Bacteria and other more advanced life forms do exist deep in Earth's oceans, where we once thought cold temperatures and extreme pressure made it impossible for anything to live. For now, however, only Earth can appropriately be called the Living Planet.

The Biosphere

For life to exist, there must be a support system for it. On Earth we call this the **biosphere**, or the life cycle. This includes the oceans, living organisms, and Earth's atmosphere. Earth has limited resources, and it constantly recycles what it has.

Ocean water evaporates into water vapor in the clouds. The clouds protect Earth from heat loss and overexposure to the Sun. They release water back to Earth as rain, snow, or other precipitation. This water falls on the land, making plant life possible, and washes minerals from the land to the oceans. As plants drop their leaves or die, they replenish the soil. This recycling is sometimes called the balance of nature.

The movement of warmth, coldness, and moisture in the air and in the oceans creates Earth's weather. The Sun does not warm all parts of the Earth equally. As warmer air

Thunderstorms loom over western Africa. These clouds are releasing water that rose to the sky in the form of vapor.

becomes thinner, it rises. As it rises, colder air moves into its place. Winds are the movements of warm and cold air. Moisture evaporates in warm air, turning into water vapor. Some of the vapor collects as clouds in the upper part of the troposphere and rides on the winds. When too much moisture accumulates, it falls as precipitation. This cycle of winds, evaporation, cloud formation, and various types of precipitation is known as the water cycle.

The balance of temperature on Earth is so fragile that small swings can cause drastic changes. When the world's average temperature lowers, water stays locked in ice and snow. Sea levels drop, and the ice caps expand. During the last ice age ten thousand years ago, glaciers extended as far south as Missouri. At that time, the average temperature was only 7°F (2.2°C) colder than it is now. When Earth's average temperature rises only a few degrees, the polar ice caps and mountain glaciers melt and the sea level rises. If all the Antarctic ice were to melt, sea levels would rise more than 200 feet (70 m). This would flood great sections of the world. Earth is currently growing warmer.

Balance Through Knowledge

In the history of humankind, especially the last ten thousand years, the design of Earth has greatly been changed. Great forests have been cut. The atmosphere is becoming polluted and chemically changed. Many plant and animal species have

People celebrate Earth Day in Washington, D.C., in 1990.

become extinct. The actions of humans will continue to affect the future of the planet, positively or negatively.

To protect life on Earth, we must keep the balance that allowed life to begin. Life as we define it demands moderate, stable temperatures, a reliable water cycle, and an atmosphere that nourishes. The greatest tool in preserving Earth is building knowledge about Earth and the universe.

We have learned much about Earth by studying the rest of the universe. In 1990, NASA launched the Hubble Space

Viewing the Stars

Our ancient ancestors could see only about 5 percent of the stars in the Milky Way. Today, the Hubble Space Telescope shows us entire galaxies, both near and distant. Shown here is a Hubble image of the beautiful Whirlpool Galaxy. Charles Messier, who first identified the Whirlpool Galaxy in 1773, described it as a very faint nebula without stars. Hubble photos show that its center is 80 light years across and has a huge concentration of more than 100 million stars around a black hole. That is five thousand times greater than the concentration of stars in the Milky Way.

The Hubble Space Telescope has brought thousands of new space objects to the human eye. This photograph shows HST in orbit around Earth in December 1993.

Telescope (HST) 380 miles (610 km) into space, away from light pollution and atmospheric distortions. HST has dramatically increased our knowledge about space. This new instrument is taking photographs of things that we never knew existed a few years ago.

Today, satellites in orbit around Earth use digital cameras and computers to measure Earth with infrared light, ultraviolet light, heat sensors, radio waves, and sound waves. The computers note changes in movement and heat and look for patterns. NASA routinely launches the space shuttle into Earth's atmosphere so that astronauts can conduct research

An infrared survey satellite orbits Earth.

and launch or repair satellites. Astronauts often take experiments designed by students into space with them to learn more about how the lack of gravity affects things.

Each new piece of knowledge teaches us that, like the scientists in the Dark Ages, we must be ready to change our assumptions. We are on a great adventure of learning, and we must look for answers from all directions. One thing will always remain true—Earth is indeed an extraordinary and exciting place.

Glossary

air pressure—the weight or push of air

atom—the smallest stable part of an element

atmosphere—the layer of gases that surrounds a planet

auroras—the effect of energy in the form of light released by gases in Earth's thermosphere after being hit by electrons from the solar winds

axis—the imaginary line around which an object rotates

barycenter—the axis on which Earth and the Moon travel around the Sun as though they were one planet

biosphere—the combination of all living organisms and their environment

comet—a ball of ice and dust that orbits around a star

density—how loosely or tightly the material in an object is packed together

galaxy—a very large group of stars rotating around a central point

gravity—the force of attraction between two objects

magma—a material made up of molten rock, crystallized minerals, and gases

magnetic field—an area in which magnetic attractions can be felt

mantle—the second layer of Planet Earth

mass—the amount of matter in an object

meteorites—rock fragments flying through space. They can measure from dust size to very large, although most are quite small. If meteorites burn up when they enter Earth's atmosphere, they are called meteors and may appear as shooting stars. If they hit the ground, they are called meteorites.

molten—melted

nebulas—giant clouds of dust particles and gases in space

orbit—to continuously move around another body in a circular or oval shape

planet—a body orbiting a star

planetesimals—lumps of dust and gases that collect together to form a planet

regolith—the layer of dust, grit, and pieces of rock that covers the Moon

rilles—long valleys or giant cracks on the Moon's surface

satellite—an object caught in the gravitational field of a larger object that it orbits

tropopause—the upper part of the troposphere

volume—the amount of space that an object takes up

water vapor—water in the form of a gas

To Find Out More

Books

Brewer, Duncan. *Planet Earth and the Universe*. New York: Marshall Cavendish, 1992.

Gallant, Roy A. *Earth's Place in Space*. Tarrytown, NY: Benchmark Books, 2000.

Graham, Ian. *The Best Book of the Moon*. New York: Kingfisher Publications, 1999.

Kelley, Kevin W., Ed. *The Home Planet*. Reading, MA: Addison-Wesley Publishing, 1988.

Redfern, Martin. *The Kingfisher Young People's Book of Planet Earth*. New York: Kingfisher Publications, 1999.

Ride, Sally and O'Shaughnessy, Tam. *The Third Planet: Exploring the Earth from Space*. New York: Crown Publishers, 1994.

Organizations and Online Sites

http://www.earth.nasa.gov
This is the official Web site for NASA's Earth division.

http://www.amnh.org/rose
This is the Web site for the American Museum of Natural History's Rose Center, with its Hall of Planet Earth (HoPE).

http://www.space.com
This site offers daily astronomy news reports and links to many sites, including a site designed for students.

Places to Visit

National Air and Space Museum
7th and Independence Avenue SW
Washington, D.C. 20560

American Museum of Natural History, Rose Center
Central Park West and 79th Street
New York, New York

A Note on Sources

When I begin to research a new book, the first thing I do is to read about my topic. I usually start with dictionaries and encyclopedias and expand to books, magazines, newspapers, and official Web sites. At the same time, I talk with anyone who has an interest in my topic to get more ideas and information.

This was an especially fun book to research. I got to go to star parties at the University of Arizona, look through the observatory's big telescopes, and talk to the astronomers. Later I went through the very impressive Rose Center Planetarium in New York City. I believe the two most important things to remember when writing nonfiction for children is to ask "why?" and "how?" I would like to thank the astronomers at the University of Arizona for their guidance, as well as my editor, Nikki Bruno, and my consultant, Margaret Carruthers, for their insight and knowledge.

—Donna Walsh Shepherd

Index

Numbers in *italics* indicate illustrations.

About the Author

Donna Walsh Shepherd has lived her whole life on Earth, but she hopes to eventually spend some of it elsewhere. When people landed on the Moon in 1969, she was in communist Hungary, where news of the landing was blocked. Two days later, in Germany, she was amazed to see the streets full of people watching televisions in store windows, rushing for newspapers, and cheering this great American accomplishment.

Currently Shepherd lives on the Pacific Ring of Fire and has experienced many earthquakes and volcanoes. She teaches writing and literature at the University of Alaska and has written several books for children.